MW00463354

LEARN BEFORE YOU LOSE

AND
FORECASTING BY TIME CYCLES

W.D.GANN

All rights reserved. No part of this publication may be reproduced, stored in a retrieval system, or transmitted in any form or by any means, electronic, mechanical, photocopying or otherwise, without the prior permission of the copyright owner.

For information regarding special discounts for bulk purchases, please contact The Richest Man in Babylon Publishing

www.therichestmaninbabylon.org

©Copyright – W.D.Gann

©Copyright 2008

www.therichestmaninbabylon.org

ALL RIGHTS RESERVED

TABLE OF CONTENTS

Why you have lost money in stocks and how to make it back

Why do the great majority of people who buy and sell stocks lose?

There are three main reasons:

1. They over-trade or buy and sell too much for their capital.

2. They do not place stop loss orders or limit their losses.

3. Lack of Knowledge. This is the most important reason of all.

Most people buy a stock because they hope it will go up and they will make profits. They buy on tips, or what someone else thinks, without any concrete knowledge of their own that the stock will advance.

Thus they entered the market wrong and did not recognize this mistake or attempt to correct it until too late.

Finally they sell because they fear the stock will go lower and often they sell out near low levels, getting out at the wrong time, making two mistakes, getting in the market at the wrong time and getting out at the wrong time. One mistake could have been prevented: they could have gotten out right after getting in wrong. They do not realize that operating in Stocks and Commodities is a business or a profession, the same as engineering or the medical profession.

WHY YOU SHOULD LEARN TO DETERMINE THE TREND OF THE MARKET

You may have tried to follow market letters and like many others either lost money or failed to make profits, because the market letters gave a list of too many stocks to buy or sell and you picked the wrong one and lost. A smart man cannot follow another man blindly even though the other man is right, because you cannot have confidence and act on advice when you do not know what it is based on. You will be able to act with confidence and make profits when you can SEE and KNOW for YOURSELF why STOCKS should go UP or DOWN. That is why you should take a Course of Instructions and prepare yourself to act independent of the advice of others.

WHY I TEACH MY METHODS

Long years in practical market trading and experience in teaching others has taught me what others need for success in speculation. They must learn a rule and how to apply it before they can take up the second lesson or set of rules. When you first went to school you had to learn your ABCs before you could read and when you started to study arithmetic you had to learn the four fundamental rules, addition, multiplication, division and subtraction. Then you were prepared to take up higher mathematics, algebra and geometry.

My Course of Lessons starts you in the same way, leading you step by step and adding more rules when you are ready and can understand them.

I have made a success in Wall Street and have all the income that I need, this fact can be proven by the records. I find real pleasure in helping others who are trying to help themselves. When I teach a young man or woman how to protect and preserve their capital I am giving them valuable knowledge that they cannot lose, and no one can steal it or take it from them.

You should never buy a method from a man who has not made money with it.

HOW YOU CAN MAKE PROFITS

You can become a successful trader or investor if you acquire knowledge and learn the mathematical rules which determine the trend of Stocks and Commodity market movements.

The Bible says: "Ye shall know the truth and the truth shall make you free." When you have learned the truth about stocks you will no longer buy on hope or sell on fear. You will face facts and be free to act on judgment based on rules that you know always have worked and always will.

WHY I CAN TEACH YOU TO SUCCEED

I have paid the price in time and money to discover, test and prove rules that are practical and get results. You will agree that 36 years experience is valuable in any line of business and that after I have spent that much time in study and research I can teach you the rules and that will take the gamble out of Stock Market trading and make it a safe and profitable business. The man who devotes all the time to any business will learn more about it than the man who only studies it a short time.

If the average man or woman would only spend the first few hundred dollars they lose in the market in acquiring knowledge and learning the rules for buying and selling at the right time, they would then make profits - not losses.

YOUR SON'S OR DAUGHTER'S FUTURE

A man can leave his son or daughter a million dollars or more and they can lose it quickly if they have not learned the rules how to invest it safely. My Course of Instructions will teach anyone how to preserve his capital and make profits. They must be willing to study and work hard.

FORECASTING BUSINESS: GOOD POSITIONS FOR STUDENTS

Changed conditions due to Government interference, regulations and changes in Europe, make it necessary for every businessman to forecast his own business in order to meet competition. It makes no difference whether a manufacturer of raw material or a seller of the finished product, he must be able to forecast future business conditions and gauge future demand as closely as possible in order to make a profit in business. This creates a good position for a man who can accurately forecast business conditions and changes. The young man who prepares himself and becomes an expert in forecasting business, Commodities, Stocks and Bonds, will find a demand for his services. Estates must have an expert to handle their investments and once a man has proven his ability to increase the profits of a large estate he will find he can name his own terms as to salary. Money must have brains and experts to increase its earning power. Large estates can and will pay a man who can keep capital intact and prevent losses. The Investment Counselor will find the future holds a bright outlook for him if he knows his business and has fully prepared himself.

WHY YOU CAN MAKE MORE PROFITS TRADING IN COMMODITIES THAN STOCKS

In trading according to my Mechanical Method & Trend Indicator or according to my 1936 New Master Forecasting Methods on Cotton, Grain, Rubber and other commodities there are many advantages over trading in stocks:

1. Commodities follow a seasonal trend and are much easier to forecast. They move with supply and demand.

2. It requires much less work to keep up charts and calculations on Commodities. There are 1200 stocks listed on the New York Stock Exchange and you must keep a separate chart on as many of them as you wish to forecast the trend of. With Cotton, you need one to three charts, and the same with Grain.

3. When you have a forecast made up for Cotton or Grain, if you are right, you are sure to make money because all options follow the same trend. There are some crosscurrents as in stocks, with some stocks declining to new low levels and others making new highs.

4. In dealing in Futures, there are no heavy interest charges as there when loss of stocks and no dividends to pay as when short of stocks.

5. Dividends can be suddenly passed or declared which will affect stock prices. This cannot happen to commodities.

6. Pools cannot manipulate a commodity as they can a stock.

7. Facts about commodities are general known while many stocks are mystery stocks all the time and some stocks are subject to false rumors.

8. The stages of the business cycle tell more about the prices of commodities than they do about stocks.

9. Commodities are governed only by demand and supply. This is not always true of stocks.

10. Speculation in commodities is more legitimate than speculation in stocks because you are dealing in a necessity.

11. Commodities are consumed. Steaks are not. This has a bearing upon forecasting commodity prices.

12. Stock prices ten to move by groups of stocks, while commodities move independently.

13. Notable speculators, like Livermore and Dr. E. H. Crawford, have discovered after long experience that they make money with greater certainty in commodities.

14. Stocks go into receivers' hands and go out of business. Commodities go on forever. Crops are planted and harvested each year.

15. There is always a demand by consumers for commodities, which is not the case with stocks.

16. Since the Securities Exchange Law was passed, marginal requirements are much higher on stocks than on Commodities. Therefore, you can make more money on the same capital trading in Cotton, Wheat, Corn, Rubber or other markets.

17. When you learn the rules for forecasting and trading in Commodities, they never change because we will always have wheat, corn, and cotton crops every year and these crops will be consumed, while stocks change and you have to study new stocks to keep up with changed conditions.

18. The price of my Commodity Methods are less than Stock Methods because it requires less time to teach them and a small number of charts are needed.

KNOWLEDGE IS POWER

Webster said: "The man who can teach me something is the man I want to know." You may think my prices are high, but stop to consider that you have the use of these Methods during you entire lifetime and that the knowledge I teach will be worth the money for one week's trading at critical times. You can easily lose in the market the price you would pay for my Course and the market leaves you with no valuable knowledge after your losses. Learn to use and know for yourself what Commodities will do; then you will make a success.

HEALTH IS WEALTH

Good health is essential for success in any business and for active trading in Stocks and Commodities. Keeping your health perfect in just as important as protecting your capital.

WHY I LIVE IN MIAMI

I have learned the value of good health and that is why I have a winter home in Miami, Florida. I give personal instruction to individuals or classes in Miami from October 1st to May 1st every year.

HOW TO TRADE

Be sure you are right before you make a trade. Never guess. Trade on scientific indications only.

WHAT YOU MUST KNOW BEFORE YOU START TRADING

You must know exactly how to apply all the rules, how to draw the geometric angles or moving-average lines from tops and bottoms; how to square Time with Price; how to bring up the important 45 degree angles or lines, which represent a moving average. You must know where to place a stop loss order and must look up what cycle the year is in, that is, determine from the Master Forecasting Chart whether it is a bull or bear year, whether the main trend should be up or down.

Before you make a trade, either buying or selling, consider the position of each individual stock on the monthly chart; next consider the weekly chart and then the daily chart. If they all confirm an uptrend, it is a cinch to buy, provided you have located the point at which to place a stop loss order. On the other hand, if the cycle shows that it is a bear year and the monthly, weekly and daily charts show downtrend, then it is the time to go short, but again you must look for the most important point - where to place the stop loss order so that it will not be more than 5 points away and closer if possible.

WHAT TO LOOK UP BEFORE YOU MAKE A TRADE

Following are the most important points that you must consider before buying or selling a stock:

1. Annual Forecast determines year of Time Cycle, whether bull or bear year, and main trend of the general market, up or down.

2. Cycle of individual stock, whether up or down year.

3. Monthly position on angles from tops and bottoms and time periods.

4. Weekly positions on time periods from tops and bottoms and on angles from tops and bottoms. See if it is squaring out Time from top or bottom.

5. Daily position on angles from important tops and bottoms and time periods. See whether a stock is near square of recent top or bottom.

6. Resistance Levels on price. See whether the stock is near any halfway point or other points of support or resistance.

7. Look to see if stock has held for several days, weeks or months around same level and whether it is about ready to cross or break important angles from tops or bottoms.

8. Look up volume of sales. See whether a stock has increased or decreased volume over past few days or weeks.

9. Look up space or price movement, up or down, for past movements. Find out what was the greatest advance or decline for past few weeks or months. For example: If a stock has reacted 5 points several times and at the time you look it up, you find it is 3 points down from the last top and the trend is up on monthly, weekly and daily with the price near a support angle, you could buy with a stop loss order 2 to 3 points away; then if the stock broke back over 5 points, the previous reaction limit, it would show a change in trend and you should be out of it.

10. Remember, the most important factor to depend on to determine the position of a stock is Geometrical Angles. Be sure to bring

up the angles from "o" from recent tops and bottoms.

11. Never overlook the fact that you must have a definite indication before making a trade.

12. Most important of all - Always locate the point at which to place a stop loss order to limit risk.

PRACTICE TRADING ON PAPER

After you feel sure that you have mastered all the rules and know exactly how to determine the trend of a stock and the place to begin trading, then to make yourself doubly sure and establish confidence, practice trading on paper until you thoroughly understand how to use the rules and when to use them. If you make mistakes trading in paper, then you would make mistakes at that time in actual trading and you are not ready to begin trading. When you feel that you are competent to start trading, apply all of the rules and *trade only on definite indications.* If you are not sure of the trend or the buying and selling price and not sure where to place a stop loss order, then wait until you get a definite indication. You can always make money by waiting for opportunities. There is no use getting in partly on guesswork and losing.

WHEN TO CLOSE A TRADE

After you start actual trading, when you make a trade, don't close it or take profits until you have a definite indication according to the rules that it is time to sell out or buy in or to move up the stop loss order and wait until it is caught. The way to make a success is to follow the trend always and not get out or close a trade until the trend changes.

WHEN TO WAIT AND NOT TRADE

It is just as important to know when not to enter the market, as it is to know when to enter it. The time not to make a trade is when you find a stick has been holding in a narrow trading range for some time, say, a 5-point or a 3-point range, but has not broken under bottoms previously made or crossed tops previously made. A stock may stay for weeks or months or even years in a trading range and will not indicate any big move or change in trend until it crosses a previous top or breaks a previous bottom. If a stick is inactive in this position it is not time to start trading in it.

Another time not to make a trade is when a stock has narrowed down between two important angles - has not broken under one or crossed the other. Wait until it gets out in the clear and gives a definite indication before you trade.

After a prolonged decline stocks nearly always narrow down and hold in a trading range for some time. Then you should wait until the angles from the bottom are broken or the angles from the top are crossed and the stock breaks over an old top before you make a trade. In other words, at all times trade when you have a definite, well-defined trend.

CAPITAL REQUIRED FOR TRADING

Before you can do any trading, you must know the amount of capital required to make a success trading and the exact amount that you must risk on any one trade in order to always have capital left to trade with.

You can begin trading in 10 shares, 100 shares, 1,000 shares or any other amount, but the main point is to divide your capital properly and to distribute the risks equally to protect your capital.

Whatever amount of capital you use to trade with, follow this rule: Divide your capital into 10 equal parts and never risk more than 10% of your capital on any one trade. Should you lose three consecutive times, then reduce your trading unit and only risk 10% of your remaining capital. If you follow this rule, your success is sure.

As a general rule, I have always considered it advisable to use at least $3,000 capital for every 100 shares of stock traded in and to limit risks to 3 points or less on every trade. In this way you will be able to make 10 trades on your capital and the market would have to beat you 10 consecutive times to wipe out your capital, which it will not do. You should try to make trades at a price where it will only be necessary to use one to two-point stop loss orders, which will cut down the risk.

If you want to start trading in small units of stock, use a capital of $300 for each 10 shares and never risk more than 3 points on the initial trade. Try to make the first trade, if possible, where your stop loss order will not be more than one or two points.

ALWAYS FOLLOW RULES: Decide this important point before you start trading. If you do not intend to follow the rules strictly, do not begin trading. Never allow guesswork or the human element to enter into your trading. Stick to the "Capital" rule and under no condition risk more than one-tenth of your capital on any one trade. Follow the mathematical rules and you will make a success.

PYRAMIDING

You should only pyramid or increase your trading in active markets where volume is above normal. The position on angles and volume of activity will show you when to pyramid. You should never begin pyramiding until a stock has gotten into a strong position on angles or into a weak position on angles, or until it has broken out of a trading range by crossing old tops or breaking old bottoms.

HOW TO PYRAMID

If you are trading in 100 shares, after you have made your first trade with a risk limited to 3 points or 10% of your capital, then do not pyramid, or buy or sell a second lot, until the market has moved at least 5 points in your favor; then when you buy or sell a second lot, use a stop loss order not more than 3 points away on both trades.

Example: We will assume that after buying the second lot, the trend reverses and the stop loss orders on both trades are caught 3 points away from where you bought the last lot. This will give you a loss of 3 points on the last trade and a profit of 2 points on the first trade, or a net loss of only one point. On the other hand, if the market continues to move in your favor, your profits will be twice as much after buying the second lot.

When the market has moved 5 points more in your favor, you buy a third lot, moving up the stop loss orders on the first and second lots and placing a stop on the entire lot of three trades not more than 3 points away and closer, if possible.

Continue to pyramid as long as the market moves 5 points in your favor, always following up with stop loss orders. When a stock selling between 5 and 75 a share has moved 15 to 25 points in your favor, you should begin to watch for a change in trend and be careful about buying or selling another lot on which you may have to take a loss.

THE RUN OR PYRAMIDING MOVE

The big money in pyramiding is made in the run between accumulation and distribution, that is, after a stock passes out of the zone of accumulation. Pyramids should be started after double or triple tops are crossed and the stock clears the zone of accumulation. Then when you get into this run, buy every 5 points up, protecting with a stop loss order not more than 3 points away from the last trade.

Reverse this rule in a declining market: After double or triple bottoms are broken and the stock clears the zone of distribution, sell every 5 points down, protecting with stop loss orders not more than 3 points above the last trade.

FAST MARKETS AND WIDE FLUCTUATIONS

When stocks are very active and moving very fast, selling above $100, then you will find it best to make trades 7 to 10 points apart. The angles and price Resistance Points as well as old tops and bottoms will determine points to place stop loss orders with safety.

In fast-moving markets, like the panic of October and November 1929, when you pyramid on active stocks and have very large profits, you should follow down, with a stop loss order about 10 points away from the market. Then, after a severe decline reduce stop loss orders, placing them about 5 points above the low level. When a market is moving as fast as this, you should not wait for the stock to go into a strong position on angles. Reverse this rule in an advancing market.

SAFEST PYRAMIDING RULE

One of the safest rules to use for pyramiding when stocks are selling at extremely high levels or extremely low levels is to start with 100 shares and when the market moves 5 points in your favor, buy another 50 shares; then when it moves 5 points or more, buy or sell 30 shares; then on the next 5-point move in your favor buy or sell 20 shares, and continue to follow the market up or down with this amount until there is a change in the main trend.

WHEN NOT TO PYRAMID

Safety is the first consideration in starting or continuing a pyramiding campaign in a stock. Mistakes are made by buying or selling a second lot too near the accumulation or the distribution point. After a big move up or down, you must always wait for a definite change in trend before starting a pyramid.

Never buy a second lot for a pyramid when a stock is near a double top or sell a second lot when a stock is near a double bottom.

A stock often holds several days or weeks in a range of 10 to 12 points, moving up and down, not crossing the highest top or breaking the last bottom made. As long as it remains in this range, you should not pyramid. When it gets out of this range, crossing the highest top or breaking the lowest bottom, then it will indicate a bigger move and you should start to pyramid.

Always check and double check, follow all the rules, study the major and minor time cycles for forecasting, the angles from tops and bottoms, the Resistance Points of Price between tops and bottoms. If you ignore one important point, it may get you wrong.

Remember, the whole can never exceed all of its parts, and all of the parts make up the whole. If you leave out one of the parts or one of the rules, you do not have a complete trend indicator.

FORECASTING BY TIME CYCLES

Time is the most important factor in determining market movements and by studying the past records of the averages or individual stocks you will be able to prove for yourself that history does repeat and that by knowing the past you can tell the future.

The ancient hunters had a rule that when they were searching to locate an animal in his den, they always followed his tracks backwards, figuring that it was the shortest route to his lair. The quickest way for you to learn how to determine future market movements is to study the past.

"The thing that hath been, it is that which shall be; and that which is done is that which shall be done, and there is no new things under the sun." Eccl. 1:9

There is a definite relation between TIME and PRICE. In previous lessons you have learned about FORMATIONS and RESISTANCE LEVELS around old tops and bottoms. Now, by a study of the TIME PERIODS and TIME CYCLES you will learn why tops and bottoms are formed at certain times and why Resistance Levels are so strong at certain times and bottoms and tops hold around them.

MAJOR TIME CYCLE

Everything moves in cycles as a result of the natural law of action and reaction. By a study of the past, I have discovered what cycles repeat in the future.

There must always be a major and a minor, a greater and a lesser, a positive and a negative. In order to be accurate in forecasting the future, you must know the major cycles. The most money is made when fast moves and extreme fluctuations occur at the end of major cycles.

I have experimented and compared past markets in order to locate the major and minor cycles and determine in what years the cycles repeat in the future. After years of research and practical tests, I have discovered that the following cycles are the most reliable to use:

10-YEAR CYCLES

The important cycle for forecasting is the cycle of around 10 years. Fluctuations of about the same nature occur which produce extreme high or low every 10 years. Stocks work out important tops and bottoms very close to the even 10-year cycle, although at times tops and bottoms come out around 10½ to 11 years in extreme markets.

The 10-year cycle equals 120 months. We divide this just the same as we divide the range between bottoms and tops to get Resistance Levels. One-half of the cycle would be 5 years or 60 months. One-fourth would be 2½ years or 30 months. One-eighth would be 15 months and one-sixteenth 7½ months. One-third would be 40 months and two-thirds of the cycle would be 80 months. All of these time periods are important to watch for changes in trend.

7-YEAR CYCLE

This cycle is 84 months. You should watch 7 years from any important top or bottom and 42 months or one-half of this cycle. You will find many culminations around the 42cd to 44th months. 21 months is one-fourth of 84 months, also important. You will find many bottoms and tops 21 to 23 months apart. At times prices make bottoms or tops 10 to 11 months from a previous top or bottom. This is due to the fact that this period is one-eighth of the 7-year cycle.

5-YEAR CYCLE

This cycle is very important because it is one-half of the 10-year cycle and the smallest complete cycle that the market works out.

MINOR CYCLES

The minor cycles are 3 years and 2 years. The smallest cycle is one year, which often shows a change in trend in the 10th or 11th month.

RULES FOR FUTURE CYCLES

Prices move in 10-year cycles, which are worked out in 5-year cycles - a 5-year cycle up and a 5-year cycle down. Begin with extreme tops and extreme bottoms to figure all cycles, either major or minor.

1. A bull campaign generally runs 5 years: 2 years up, 1 year down, and 2 years up, completing a 5-year cycle. The end of a 5-year campaign comes in the 59th or 60th month. Always watch for the change in the 59th month.

2. A bear cycle often runs 5 years down - the first move 2 years down, then 1 year up, and 2 years down, completing the 5-year downswing.

3. Bull or bear campaigns seldom run more than 3 to 3½ years up or down without a move of 3 to 6 months or one year in the opposite direction, except at the end of Major Cycles, like 1869 and 1929. Many campaigns culminate in the 23rd month, not running out the full 2 years. Watch the weekly and monthly charts to determine whether the culmination will occur in the 23rd, 24th, 27th or 30th month of the move, or in extreme campaigns in the 34th to 35th or 41st to 42nd month.

4. Adding 10 years to any top, it will give you the top of the next 10-year cycle, repeating about the same average fluctuations.

5. Adding 10 years to any bottom, it will give you the bottom of the next 10-year cycle, repeating the same kind of a year and about the same average fluctuations.

6. Bear campaigns often run out in 7-year cycles, or 3 and 4 years from any complete bottom. From any complete bottom of a cycle, first add 3 years to get the next bottom; then add 4 years to that bottom to get bottom of a 7-year cycle. For example: 1914 bottom - add 3 years, gives 1917, low of panic; then add 4 years to 1917, gives 1921, low of another depression.

7. To any final major or minor top, add 3 years to get the next top; then add 3 years to that top, which will give you the third top; add 4 years to the third top to get the final top of a 10-year cycle. Sometimes a change in trend from any top occurs before the end of the regular time period, therefore you should begin to watch the 27th, 34th, and 42nd months for a reversal.

8. Adding 5 years to any top, it will give the next bottom of a 5-year cycle. In order to get top for the next 5-year cycle, add 5 years to

any bottom. For example: 1917 was bottom of a big bear campaign; add 5 years give 1922, top of a minor bull campaign. Why do I say " Top of a minor bull campaign"? Because the major bull campaign was due to end in 1929.

1919 was top; adding 5 years to 1919 gives 1924 as bottom of a 5-year bear cycle. Refers to Rules 1 and 2, which tell you that a bull or bear campaign seldom runs more than 2 to 3 years in the same direction. The bear campaign from 1919 was 2 years down - 1920 and 1921; therefore, we only expect one-year rally in 1922; then 2 years down - 1923 and 1924, which completed the 5-year bear cycle.

Looking back to 1913 and 1914, you will see that 1923 and 1924 must be bear years to complete the 10-year cycle from the bottoms of 1913-1914. Then, note 1917 bottom of a bear year; adding 7 years gives 1924 also as bottom of a bear cycle. Then, adding 5 years to 1924 gives 1929 top of a cycle.

1913 1914.

07 1
08
092
10 3
11 4   47
12 5

FORECASTING MONTHLY MOVES

Monthly moves can be determined by the same rules as yearly:

Add 3 months to an important bottom, then add 4, making 7, to get minor bottoms and reaction points.

In big upswings a reaction will often not last over 2 months, the third month being up, the same rule as in yearly cycle - 2 down and the third up.

In extreme markets, a reaction sometimes only lasts 2 or 3 weeks; then the advance is resumed. In this way a market may continue up for 12 months without breaking a monthly bottom.

In a bull market the minor trend may reverse and run down 3 to 4 months; then turn up and follow the main trend again.

In a bear market, the minor trend may run up to 3 to 4 months, then reverse and follow the main trend, although, as a general rule, stocks never rally more than 2 months in a bear market; then start to break in the third month and follow the main trend down.

NATURAL SEASONAL TIME CHANGES

While we do not use the calendar months for time periods, unless an extreme high or low should occur around January 2 or 3rd, we do use the Seasonal Time Periods which are more important and many of the important highs and lows have occurred around these Seasonal Time Periods. These periods are as follows:

December 21, any year *WINTER EQINOX.*

February 5

May 5

June 21 *SUMMER EQINOA*

August 5

September 21 *FAll EQUINOX.*

November 8

Then repeat, December 21, etc., for the 2nd and 3rd years.

These Seasonal Time Periods divide the year into 8 equal parts of approximately 45 days each. You can divide these time periods into 2 equal parts which are approximately 22½ days. Example: December 21 to February 5 gives January 13 as the ½ period, and between June 21 to August 5 is July 14.

49

The variation from these Time Periods is usually 3 to 4 days before or after the actual dates. The most important in Grains occur during FEBRUARY, MAY, AUGUST and NOVEMBER, therefore: these days and months are the most important to watch for major changes in trend, but always keep in mind the dates of the previous highs and lows of past years and watch for the change in trend around these dates.

Mr. W. D. GANN

THIRTY-ONE YEARS IN WALL STREET

The Founder and president of W. D. Gann & Son, Inc., has devoted 35 years exclusively to the study of stock and commodity markets and has spent over $300,000.00 developing a worthwhile, practical method of Stock Forecasting.

During the past years, W. D. Gann has been in business for himself and under his own name in New York City. He is a member of the Commodity Exchange, Inc. of New York, New Orleans Cotton Exchange and is a Christian and a member of the Masonic fraternity.

THE RECORD OF FORECASTS - HIGHLIGHTS THROUGH THE YEARS

1909 - W. D. Gann's record as a forecaster dates back 30 years. We reprint part of an article written by the late Richard D. Wyckoff and published in the Ticker Magazine. This article is dated December 1909 and attests to Mr. Gann's remarkable ability as a forecaster over 30 years ago.

WILLIAM D. GANN - An Operator Whose Science and Ability Place Him in the Front Rank - His Remarkable Predictions and Trading Record

Sometime ago the attention of this magazine was attracted by certain long pull stock market predictions which were being made by William D. Gann. In a large number of cases Mr. Gann gave us in advance the exact points of which certain stocks and commodities would sell, together with prices close to the then prevailing figures which would not be touched.

For instance, when New York Central was 131 he predicted that it would sell at 145 before 129.

So repeatedly did his figures prove to be accurate, and so different did his work appear from that of any expert whose methods we had examined, that we set about to investigate Mr. Gann and his way of figuring out these predictions, an well as the particular use which he was making of them in the market.

The results of this investigation are remarkable in many ways. It appears to be a fact that Mr. Gann has developed an entirely new idea as to the principles governing stock market movements. He bases his operations upon certain natural laws, which, though existing since the world began, have only in recent years been subjected to the will of man and added to the list of so-called modern discoveries.

We have asked Mr. Gann for an outline of his work and have secured some remarkable evidence as to the results obtained therefrom. We submit this in full recognition of the fact that in Wall Street a man with a new idea - an idea which violates the traditions and encourages a scientific view of the proposition - is not usually welcomed by the majority, for the reason that he stimulates thought and research. These activities said majority abhors.

Mr. Gann's description of his experience and methods is given herewith. It should be read with a recognition of the established fact that Mr. Gann's predictions have proved correct in a large majority of instances.

"After years of patient study I have proven to my entire satisfaction as well as demonstrated to others that vibration explains every possible phase of the market."

In order to substantiate Mr. Gann's claims as to what he has been able to do under this method, we called upon Mr. William E. Gilley, an Inspector of Imports, 16 Beaver Street, New York. Mr. Gilley is well known in the downtown district. He himself has studied stock market movements for twenty-five years, during which time he has examined every piece of market literature that has been issued and procurable in Wall Street. It was he who encouraged Mr. Gann to study out the scientific and mathematical possibilities of the subject. When asked what had been the most impressive of Mr. Gann's work and predictions, he replied as follows:

"It is very difficult for me to remember all the predictions and operations of Mr. Gann which may be classed as phenomenal, but the following are a few: In 1908 when Union Pacific was 168⅛ he told me that it would not touch 169 before it had a good break. We sold it short all the way down to 152⅝, covering on the weak spots and putting it out again on the rallies, securing twenty-three points profit out of an eighteen-point move.

"He came to me when United States Steel was selling around 50 and said, 'This Steel will run up to 58 but it will not sell at 59. From there it should break 16¾ points. We sold it short around 58⅜ with a stop at 59.

The highest it went was 58¾. From there it declined to 41¼ - 17½ points.

"At another time wheat was selling at about 89c. He predicted that the May option would sell at $1.35. We bought it and made large profits on the way up. It actually touched $1.35½.

"When Union Pacific was 172, he said it would go to 184⅞ but not an eighth higher until it had had a good break. It went to 184⅞ and came back from there eight or nine times. We sold it short repeatedly with a stop at 185 and were never caught. It eventually came back to 177½.

"Mr. Gann's calculations are based on natural law. I have followed his work closely for years. I know that he has a firm grasp of the basic principles which govern stock market movements, and I do not believe any other man on earth can duplicate the idea or his method at the present time.

"Early this year he figured that the top of the advance would fall on a certain day in August and calculated the prices at which the Dow-Jones Averages would then stand. The market culminated on the exact day and within four-tenths of one per cent of the figures predicted."

"You and Mr. Gann must have cleaned up considerable money on all these operations," was suggested.

"Yes, we have made a great deal of money. He has taken half a million dollars out of the market in the past few years. I once saw him take $130, and in less than one month run it up to cover $12,000. He can compound money faster than any man I ever met."

"One of the most astonishing calculations made by Mr. Gann was during the last summer (1909) when he predicted that September wheat would sell at $1.20. This meant that it must touch that figure before the end of the month of September. At twelve o'clock, Chicago time, on September 30th (the last day) the option was selling below $1.08, and it looked as though his prediction would not be fulfilled. Mr. Gann said, 'If if does not touch $1.20 before the close of the market it will prove that there is something wrong with my whole method of calculation. I do not care what the price is now, it must go there.' It is common history that September wheat surprised the whole country by selling at $1.20 and no higher in the very last hour of the trading, closing at that figure.

So much for what Mr. Gann has said and done is evidenced by himself and others. Now as to what demonstrations have taken place before our representative:

During the month of October 1909, in twenty-five market days, Mr. Gann made, in the presence of our representative, two hundred and eighty-six transactions in various stocks, on both the long and short side of the market. Two hundred and sixty-four of these transactions resulted in profits, twenty-two in losses.

The capital with which he operated was doubled ten times, so that at the end of the month he had one thousand per cent of his original margin.

In our presence, Mr. Gann sold Steel common short at 94⅞, saying that it would not do 95. It did not.

On a drive which occurred during the week ending October 29th, Mr. Gann bought Steel common at 86¼, saying that it would not go to 86. The lowest it sold was 86⅛.

We have seen him give in one day sixteen successive orders in the same stock, eight of which turned out to be either the top or the bottom eighth of that particular swing. The above we can positively verify.

Such performances as these, coupled with the foregoing, are probably unparalleled in the history of the Street.

James R. Keene has said, "The man who is right six times out of ten will make his fortune." Here is a trader who, without any attempt to make a showing (for he did not know the results were to be published), establishes a record of over ninety-two per cent profitable trades.

Mr. Gann has refused to disclose his method at any price, but to those scientifically inclined he has unquestionably added to the stock of Wall Street knowledge and pointed out infinite possibilities.

We have requested Mr. Gann to figure out for the readers of The Ticker a few of the most striking indications which appear in his calculations. In presenting these we wish it understood that no man, in or out of Wall Street, is infallible.

Mr. Gann's figures at present indicate that the trend of the stock market should, barring the usual rallies, be toward lower prices until March or April 1910.

He calculates that May wheat, which is now selling at $1.02, should not sell below 99c and should sell at $1.45 next spring.

On cotton, which is now at about the 15c-level, he estimates that after a good reaction from these prices, the commodity should reach 18c in the spring of 1910. He looks for a corner in the March or May option.

Whether these figures prove correct or not, will in no sense detract from the record which Mr. Gann has already established.

Mr. Gann was born in Lufkin, Texas, and is thirty-one years of age. He is a gifted mathematician, has an extraordinary memory for figures, and is an expert Tape Reader. Take away his science and he would beat the market on his intuitive tape reading alone.

Endowed as he is with such qualities, we have no hesitation in predicting that within a comparatively few years, W. D. Gann will receive full recognition as one of Wall Street's leading operators.

Note: Since the above forecast was made, Cotton has suffered the expected decline, the extreme break having been 120 points. The lowest on May wheat thus far has been $1.01⅝. It is now selling at 1.06¼. In 1912 Mr. Gann forecast the election of Woodrow Wilson and had been correct in forecasting the election of every President since that time. Many of these forecasts have been published in newspapers throughout the country.
In the spring of 1918 Mr. Gann forecast the end of the World War. This forecast was sent out to newspapers throughout the country, and in January 1919, the New York Herald and other papers gave Mr. Gann credit for forecasting the end of the war and the Kaiser's abdication.
In his 1919 Annual Stock Forecast, issued late in 1918, he forecast a big bull market for 1919 and especially referred to a boom in oil stocks.

His Stock Forecasts for 1920 and 1921 indicated a bear market with sharp declines. The 1921 Forecast called the exact date for bottom on stocks in August 1921.

In 1923 Mr. Gann wrote "Truth of the Stock Tape" and forecast a big advance in chemical and airplane stocks, which followed during the Coolidge bull campaign. This book has been reviewed by newspapers and magazines throughout the country and favorably commented on by college professors, businessmen, investors and traders, all of who agree that it is the best book ever written on the subject.

His Stock Forecasts for 1924 and 1925 outlined the bull market which followed.

In the spring of 1927, Mr. Gann wrote "The Tunnel Thru the Air, or Looking Back From 1940," which contained many remarkable forecasts in regard to stocks and commodities and world events which have been fulfilled. In this book Mr. Gann said that from 1929 to 1932 there would be the worst panic in the world's history. Writing under date of "October 3, 1931" on page 323, he said, "The New York Stock Exchange closed to prevent complete panic because the people were panic-stricken and selling stocks regardless of price." It is a matter of history that the New York Stock Exchange did consider closing on October 3

66

to5, but decided to stop short selling. The low of that panicky decline was reached on October 5 and a rally of 33 points in industrial stock averages followed to November 9, 1931.

His 1929 Stock Forecast, issued on November 23, 1928, and based on his Master Time Factor, indicated the end of the full market in August and early September 1929. He stated in no uncertain terms that the panic would start in September 1929, and that it would be a great deluge with a Black Friday. We quote from the Forecast:

"AUGUST - A few of the late movers will advance this month and reach final high. ***Unfavorable news will develop which will start declines and the long bull campaign will come to a sudden end. Money rates will be high and final top will be reached for a big bear campaign. Stand from under! Don't get caught in the great deluge! Remember it is too late to sell when everyone is trying to sell.***

"SEPTEMBER - One of the sharpest declines of the year is indicated. There will be loss of confidence by investors, and the public will try to get out after it is too late. Storms will damage crops and the general business outlook will become cloudy. War news will upset the market and unfavorable developments in foreign countries. A 'Black Friday' is indicated and a panicky decline in stocks with only small rallies. The short side will prove the most profitable. You should sell short and pyramid on the way down."

In the spring of 1930, Mr. Gann wrote "Wall Street Stock Selector," which was published in June 1930. In this book he had a chapter headed, "Investors' Panic," which described conditions just as they occurred during 1931, 1932 and 1933. We quote from the book, pages 203-04:

"The coming investors' panic will be the greatest in history, because there are at least 15 to 25 million investors in the United States who hold stocks in the leading corporations, and when once they get scared, which they will after years of decline, then the selling will be so terrific that no buying power can withstand it. Stocks are so well distributed in the hands of the public that since the 1929 panic many people think that the market in panic-proof, but this seeming strength is really the weakest feature of the market.

"Love of money has been the cause of all financial troubles and depressions in the past, and the coming panic will be the greatest the world has ever known, because there is more money in the United States than ever before, therefore more to fight for."

Thousands of people have bought this book and profited by reading and studying it. The book had been favorably commented on by such papers as The Financial Times of London, England, Wall Street Journal, New York Daily Investment News, Coast Investor, and many other newspapers and magazines throughout the world.

On February 10, 1932, Mr. Gann said that stocks were bottom for a big rally. His 1932 Stock Forecast, issued October 21, 1931, called March 8 for last top for another big decline. During the latter part of June 1932 and early July, he strongly advised buying stocks, stating that final bottom had been reached, as shown by his market letter issued July 8, the day that most stocks reached final bottom. We quote from page 6 of the 1932 Forecast:

"The latter part of June, July, August and September are the most active and bullish months of the year, when sharp advances will be recorded. First extreme high is indicated around September 20 to 21, when stocks should make extreme high for the year. Then follows a decline, reaching bottom around October 4 to 5."

Between July 8 and September 8 many stocks advanced 20 to 60 points. The market reached high of a secondary rally on September 23, from which a big decline followed, making low in the latter part of November and early December, as indicated in the Forecast.

On March 1, 1933, by the use of his Master Time Factor, Mr. Gann forecast bottom for stocks and commodities and advised buying for a big advance, as shown by the market letters issued March 1 and 3 given below. This is another proof of the great value of Mr. Gann's discovery of a Master Time Factor.

KEEPING UP TO DATE

Mr. Gann has always been progressive and believes in keeping up to date. In April 1933, he bought a specially equipped airplane for making crop surveys. Many of the newspapers throughout the country commented on this progressive step. The following article appeared in the New York Daily Investment News, May 26, 1933:

NEW YORK DAILY INVESTMENT NEWS GANN TO TOUR COUNTRY BY PLANE FOR BROAD BUSINESS SURVEY

Wayne, Mich., May 25 --W. D. Gann, stock market analyst, of 99 Wall St., today left here for New York with the first 1933 model Stinson Reliant plane, piloted by Elinor Smith, woman aviator.

Mr. Gann will use the plane for an extensive tour of the country during which he will study cotton, wheat and tobacco crop and business conditions. He will leave on this tour early in June.

The forecaster expects to make speed in the gathering of firsthand information on business conditions by use of the airplane.

The plane is equipped with blind-flying apparatus, extra-large fuel tanks to afford a flying range of 750 miles and with radio receiving equipment. The plane is powered with a Lycoming engine and is capable of 135 miles per hour.

By receiving radio advices on market conditions, Mr. Gann calculates that he will be able at all times to gauge his operations in the markets and send up-to-the-minute advice to his clients, even though he is many miles away from his Wall Street office.

As far as is known, Mr. Gann will be the first Wall Street adviser to use a plane as part of his equipment in studying market conditions.

The recent burst of activity in the markets, following the closing of the banks and leading stock and commodity exchanges, prompted the analyst to buy the plane.

He decided that rapid-changing conditions made it necessary for him to gather his data on crops and business at firsthand.

Mr. Gann is a member of the Commodity Exchange, Inc., and also of the New Orleans Cotton Exchange. During his tour of the country he will visit the cotton belt in the south and southwest, the tobacco fields in the south, and the wheat stand in the middle west.

At all times during the trip he will communicate regularly with his office by wire and by radio. He expects to make talks in various cities to Kiwanis and Rotary Clubs, chambers of commerce and other business organizations.

His itinerary will include the following cities:

Washington, D.C.; Richmond, Va.; Raleigh, N.C.; Atlanta, Ga.; Birmingham, Ala.; Memphis, Tenn.; New Orleans, La.; Little Rock, Ark.; Houston and Dallas, Texas; St. Louis, Detroit and Chicago.

1933 STOCK FORECAST

Mr. Gann's 1933 Stock Forecast called for top July 17 and a sharp decline to July 21. Stocks reached high on July 17 and a wide-open break followed, with the average down 25 points in 4 days.

1934 STOCK FORECAST

His 1934 Forecast indicated top for February 13th and the high was reached on averages February 5th and 15th. The next low was indicated for May 11th to 12th, and the market made low on May 14th. The next top was indicated for June 22nd; stocks reached high on June 19th. The last low for 1934 was forecast for July 21st to 23rd and the extreme low of the year was reached on July 26th. The Forecast called for the last top for September 8th to 10th, and stocks reached top of the rally on September 6th. A reaction followed to September 17th, the exact date indicated in the Forecast for low. The next top was forecast for October 5th and 6th and the industrial averages reached top October 11th. The next bottom was called for October 23rd to 24th and the lows were reached October 26th. The next top was indicated, according to the Forecast, for December 4th to 5th. The averages reached top on December 6th and a reaction followed. The Forecast indicated high for the end of December and the averages reached high for the month on December 31st.

A CROP SURVEY IN SOUTH AMERICA

In the early part of March 1935, Mr. Gann made a trip to South America to study crop conditions and get firsthand information on the increase in population of cotton in Peru, Chile, Argentine, and Brazil. On this trip he covered about 18,000 miles by airplane and more than 1,000 miles by automobile, driving into the country to see the conditions of soil and the possibilities for increased production of Wheat, Corn and Cotton, which will influence prices in the United States market by underselling, due to lower cost of labor in Argentine and Brazil. While in South America, Mr. Gann was interviewed by many newspapers.

We reproduce part of an article which appeared in the Beunos Aires Herald, March 21, 1935.

SCIENCE AND STOCK
An astonishing Claims
Records of 1,000 Years

The man who guesses and gambles on hope is sure to lose while the man who follows science makes profits. There is cause and effect for everything and by time element and the cycle theory everything can be mathematically determined.

Mr. W. D. Gann, member of the New Orleans Cotton Exchange and the Rubber Exchange of New York, who stated that he had devote over 30 years to study of time cycles and spent $300,000 (U.S.) to develop a dependable method based on mathematical science that will determine the trend of stocks and commodities. The success attending his methods, he asserts, are borne out by his own good fortune on the American markets, and his accuracy in forecasting the futures markets for the past twenty years has been very widely commented upon in the Press in all parts of the United States.

Mr. Gann told a HERALD reporter yesterday that he has carried his records of grain back over 1,000 years and cotton records nearly 400 years. The former he was able to gather the most accurate information about from old British records, while in search for cotton cycles he visited Egypt and India. More recently he has used his own aeroplane extensively in America for getting round the country quickly to make forecasts on the cotton crops.

1935 STOCK FORECAST:

His 1935 Forecast indicated top for January 9th to 10th and the high was reached on January 7th. The next top was forecast for February 13th. The actual highs were reached February 18th, from which a sharp decline followed, making low for the year on March 18th. The Forecast called for the last low on March 28th, and the averages made a second low on March 25th. From the low in March, the Forecast indicated a big advance of at least 32 points in the Dow-Jones Industrial Averages.

August 28th and 29th indicated top for a reaction. The averages reached top on

August 27th and then reacted. The Forecast called for the next top September 12th to 15th. High on the averages was reached September 11th. The Forecast indicated the next bottom for September 24th to 25th; the last low was made September 20th and 26th.

The Forecast called for top October 26th to 28th, and the averages reached high on October 28th, which was the high of the year up to that time. The Forecast indicated November 15th to 16th as the last high of the year. The actual high of the Dow-Jones 30 Industrial Averages was reached on November 20th, from which a reaction of 10 points on averages followed. The Forecast called for low December 9-10th and 23rd. The low of the reaction was made on December 16th and 19th. The Forecast called for a rally to December 31st, and this rally took place.

Mr. Gann has also been issuing Annual Forecast on Cotton, Wheat and other commodities for many years. These Forecasts have shown the same percentage of accuracy that the Stock Forecasts have.

These Annual Forecasts on Stocks, Cotton and Grain are issued in October and November each year for the following year.

NEW STOCK TREND DETECTOR

In December 1935, Mr. Gann wrote a new book, NEW STOCK TREND DETECTOR*, bringing "Wall Street Stock Selector" up-to-date, with new rules never before published and a method of trading that formerly sold for $1,000. This book covers changed conditions caused by the new Securities Exchange laws. It gives an example of trading in Chrysler Motors from 1925 to the end of 1935 and new rules on Volume of Sales. This book with the two former books will give you a valuable stock market education.

---

* Avalaible at www.therichestmaninbabylon.org

W. D. GANN MAKES PROFITS TRADING ACCORDING TO HIS OWN METHODS

Many ask the question, "If Mr. Gann can forecast the market accurately, why does he sell service or write market letters?" He has answered that question before, that he finds pleasure in giving his knowledge to help others who need help; money is not everything in life.

Below we publish a record taken from brokers' statements, showing the trades made by Mr. Gann for 3 years. This is proof that he can and does make money by following his own rules and methods. Before you buy a course of instructions, get the record of actual trading by the man who is behind it. If he has not made money following his own advice, why should you pat money for it and follow it and risk your money?

W. D. GANN'S TRADING RECORD FOR 1933

From August 1 to December 31:
Total number of traded - _135_ - of which 112 showed profits and 23 losses.
Percentage of accuracy on the total number of trades: 83%
Percentage of profits to losses: 89.9%
Total number of trades for the entire year of 1933: 479 trades, of which 422 were profits and 57 showed losses.
Percentage of accuracy: 88.1%
Percentage of profits on capital used: 4000% or 40 for 1

TRADING RECORD FOR 1934

From January 1 to December 31:
Total number of trades: _362_
Cotton: 147 trades, of which 135 showed profits and 12 losses.
Grain: 170 trades, of which 161 showed profits and 9 losses.
Rubber: 23 trades, of which 21 showed profits and 2 losses.
Silver: 7 trades, of which 7 showed profits and 0 loss.
Silk: 4 trades, of which 3 showed profits and 1 loss.

Stocks: 11 trades, of which 10 showed profits and 1 loss.

Total for year, 362, of which 337 showed profits and 25 losses.

Percentage of accuracy on the total number of trades: 93.09%

Percentage of profits to losses: 93.10%

Percentage of profits on capital used: 800% or 8 for 1

TRADING RECORD FOR 1935

Commodities:

Total trades in Cotton, Grain and Rubber - 98 - of which 83 showed profits and 15 showed losses.

Percentage of accuracy on total number of trades: 85%

Percentage of profits to losses: 82%

Percentage of profits on capital used: 336%

Stocks:

Total number trades - 34- of which 29 showed profits and 5 losses.

Percentage of accuracy on total number of trades: 85.5%

Percentage of profits to losses: 83%

Percentage of profits on capital used: 100%

Such a record of accuracy proves that W. D. Gann has discovered a Master Time Factor and Cycle Theory that works and can be depended upon in future.

1936

"New Stock Trend Detector" was written by W. D. Gann. This book was a further advance over "Truth of the Stock Tape" and "Wall Street Stock Selector" and contained an actual trading record for 10 years in Chrysler Motors according to the rules set down in these books.

Bought Special built all-metal Airplane, "The Silver Star" for making crop survey.

1937

Wrote and published a book, "How to Make Profits Trading in Puts and Calls". Scientific Stock Forecasting again proved equal to the text of predicting a bear year, sharp declines coming in March and September. A maximum decline of 80 points was called for and the actual decline from the March high to the November low was 82 and a fraction points. We reprint an article from the Milwaukee Journal giving further details.

PREDICTED STOCK MARKET CRASHES OF 1929, 1937

Gann Says There'll Be Another Decline in November and an Upturn in December of This Year

NEW YORK, N.Y. - W. D. Gann, who forecast the 1929 stock market crash one year in advance and predicted the exact date, September 3, 1929, when the panic would start, has made another kill.

His 1937 Stock Forecast, issued November 18, 1936, is just as accurate. On page 2 he said - General Outlook for 1937:

"This year comes under a time cycle which definitely indicates a bear year in most stocks and a panicky decline in the first half of the year and another panicky decline in the last half of the year. Fluctuations will be wide. Sudden, unexpected events of an unfavorable nature will occur from time to time which will upset the market and rallies will fail to hold. Action by the government and laws changed or passed by Congress will have a great influence on business conditions and stock prices.

"Many people are still buying stocks or holding stocks and hoping for the day when inflation will come and they will be able to sell at high prices. Inflation has been going on ever since 1933 and one of these days people will wake up and find that deflation has set in and then they will realize that inflation had already existed.

"The Securities and Exchange Commission is getting more drastic in its regulations of operations on the Exchange and there is likely to be more legislation in 1937. This will cause less support to the market in the future because there will be less buying by floor traders and specialists, and probably less short selling, therefore less support from short sellers when a panic takes place. The final result of all the regulation is likely to do more harm than good as far as the public is concerned."

A MATTER OF RECORD

It is a matter of record that the Dow-Jones 30 Industrial stock averages reached extreme high on March 8, 1937, and Mr. Gann's forecast called March 6-8 as last high of the year. The decline lasted until June 18, when the Dow-Jones averages were down 32 points. His forecast called for a decline of 32 points and indicated June 23-25 as last low before a rally into August. The forecast said last high would be reached August 25-27 before a panicky decline would start. The Dow-Jones averages reached high August 14, up 27 points from June lows, and on August 25 the market had the last rally and the decline started.

LONG BEAR WAVE

In his forecast for August on page 15 he said: "This should be one of the active months for the stock market. Sudden, unexpected events of an unfavorable nature will cause some sharp breaks and, in fact, this is the month when the market should start on its long bear wave again. The newspapers will try to make it appear that business is improving but it will be far from good. There will be disturbing conditions at Washington and some trouble over crop control or shortage of crops due to government action. Stocks will rally from time to time but the short side is where the big money will be made."

The bear market started in August as predicted. Mr. Gann's forecast called for low October 14-15 and the extreme lows were reached on October 19, just four days later, when there was a panicky decline, culmination in one of the worst declines in the history of the stock exchange, with the Dow-Jones Averages down 79.65 points. The most uncanny prediction by Mr. Gann was that the averages could decline a maximum of 80 points.

In his 1937 forecast, page 7, he said: "The range in these industrial averages during 1937 is not likely to be less than 50 to 60 points and may reach a maximum of 80 points."

His forecast called for a sharp advance from October 15 to 30 and the Dow-Jones Averages advanced 25 points from October 19 to 30.

ADVANCE IN DECEMBER

Mr. Gann was asked how it was possible to make such an accurate forecast one year in advance. He stated that it was his own discovery of a mathematical master time factor and cycle theory which enables him to tell when certain cycles recur and great panics and booms take place. He said that the extent of an advance was determined by a theory based on the law of averages and that under certain circumstances stocks decline or advance about the same number of points.

"What about the near future of the stock market?" Gann replied: "My forecast indicates that the stocks will back and fill until around November 15, when Congress meets. Then they will have another decline and reach low of the reaction about November 26-27, followed by an advance in December."

1938

Predicted bull market to start in the spring or early summer, and called for low of the year for the early part of April. Actual low occurred on March 31st. This Forecast strongly advised buying airplane stocks and said they would lead the market upward. It is now market history that the airplane stocks as a group were the strongest on the New York Stock Exchange, and many of these stocks doubled and tripled in value during 1938.

AGAIN, WE REPEAT:

"Prove all things and hold fast to that which is good."

1939

The Stock Forecast called for high January 3rd, the Dow-Jones Industrial Averages made high January 4th and started to decline.
The Forecast indicated low for January 21st to 23rd, the averages reached low January 26th.
February 4th to 6th indicated high, averages made high February 6th.
February 21st to 23rd indicated low, averages made low February 21st.
March 4th to 6th indicated high, averages made high March 10th.
March 8th to 9th and 24th to 25th indicated low, averages made low March 22nd and 28th.
April 19th to 20th called for last low, averages made low April 11th.

May 16th-17th indicated high, averages made high May 10th to 15th.

June 7th to 9th indicated high, averages made high June 9th, and a sharp decline followed.

June 23rd to 24th indicated low, averages made low June 29th to 30th.

July 28th to 29th indicated high, averages made high July 25th to 28th.

August 4th to 5th indicated low, averages made low August 5th and 7th.

The 1939 Forecast was issued and mailed to subscribers on November 14th, 1938.

We are sure that anyone will agree that such accurate, long-range forecasting cannot be done by guesswork. You can learn to make forecasts one year or more in advance when you learn how to apply the rules taught with the Master Forecasting Method.

WHAT OTHERS SAY OF W. D. GANN'S METHODS:

Below we print copies of letters from two prominent businessmen, many other letters on file in our office from people who have used Mr. Gann's Courses of Instruction and followed his advice.

New York, N.Y.
March 16, 1933.

My Dear Mr. Gann:

I am very glad to write you a letter stating my personal observations of the application of your system to trading in Cotton.

On November 30, 1923, starting with a capital of $973.00, you showed a clear profit of over $30,000 at the close of business on January 28, 1924. This profit was made through the purchase and sale of contracts for the delivery and sale of cotton on the New York Cotton Exchange through one of the leading New York brokerage offices. I personally know of all the trades made in this community for the account, having received advices of your operations from the broker on the day following the day each trade was made.

On January 29, 1924, a check for $24,764.04 was drawn against the account and delivered to a person with whom I am personally acquainted.

- C. M.

****

New Bern, N.C.
August 23rd, 1937

I have known Mr. W. D. Gann for many years. I have been in his office on Wall Street, have seen him trade with his method and take the money out of the market. With it he has made a fortune in speculation. And he does not need the money he gets for his method service any more than Mr. Ford does for sale of cars.

His method has been used by me successfully since 1927. In my opinion, it is the only one with which one can make money in the market and keep it. If you will follow his method and the rules he lays down, you will also make a success and I can assure you without it you will make a failure.

This statement is made after having read every book I could find on the subject, including the lives of all the big operators of the past and subscribed to every financial paper published and most of the market services.

- C. K.

RESULTS OF TRADING ACCORDING TO THE RULES

One of the rules is for trading in fast moves after the market gives a definite signal for a big move up or down. This rule gets you in the market when activity starts and keeps you in until the move has run its course, enabling you to make large profits in a comparatively short period of time.

Trading in the Dow-Jones 30 Industrial Averages beginning June 5th, 1897 to July 25th, 1939 you would have been in the market 1,238 weeks or 24 1/3 years out of a total of 42 years.

Total number of points profit would have been:

2,367

Average points profit per month:

1.84

Profits on 100 shares of stock would have been:

$236,700.00
(without pyramiding or ever trading in more than 100 shares)

Figures do not allow for errors in judgment, commission or interest, making a liberal deduction of 25% to cover same:

$59,175.00

Net profit on 100 shares, or a capital of $3,000:

$177,525.00

You could have started trading in 1897 in 100 shares on a capital of $1,000.00 but according to the methods and rules you should have started with a capital of $3,000.00 for trading in 100 shares.

Should you have traded in the active leading stocks at all times, instead of the averages, the profits would have been much greater because the active leaders moved from one to three times as many points as the average.

Dow-Jones 20 Railroad Averages May 1897 to March 1914 and Dow-Jones Industrial Averages February 1913 to June 1939, trading according to the rules during the above periods, show possible points:

Advances:

2,085.52

Possible decline

2,012.42

Total points:

4097.94

Points made on Advance:

1,336.78

Points made on Decline:

1,236.13

Total:

2,572.91

Percentage of total points made to possible total points: 63%
Percentage of total points made on the upside or Bull Market: 64%
Percentage of total points made on the downside or Bear Market: 61.4%

Total number of trades made:

177

Total number years:

42

Average number of trades per year

4.2

(Slightly above 4 per year)

Net profit per year on 100 shares:

$6,125.74

Net profit on 100 shares from 1897 to 1939:

$257,291.00

Figuring an original investment of:

$5,000.00

Equity as of June 30th, 1939 would be:

$262,291.00

Value of $199 invested in 1897 as of June 1939: $5,145.82

www.therichestmaninbabylon.org

www.therichestmaninbabylon.org

Printed in the United States
152553LV00002B/8/P

9 789650 060084